insp**HIRE**d

novel ideas for novel leaders

Brian Parsley

Lito Press
Charlotte

Published by Lito Press, Charlotte, NC.

To order additional copies of this title, call 704-333-1112.
The author may be contacted at the following address:
Brian Parsley
310 Arlington Ave, Loft 329
Charlotte, NC 28203
Phone 704-333-1112, Fax 704-333-1011
Email: brian@trainone.com
Web site: www.brianparsley.com

Cover Design by Josh Gitomer
Page design by David Beard

Printed in the United States.
ISBN 1-59975-014-7

To my wife, Jennifer,
who makes my life worth living.
You give me the strength and
encouragement to always do what is right.
I am grateful for your support.

To my daughter, Alexis.
You are our miracle child!
You are my inspiration and I will never
be able to tell you I love you enough.

Brian Parsley is attractive.

He's not pretty. In fact, he's borderline ugly – but he's attractive in personality, style, demeanor and attitude. Those are the qualities of a leader. And those are the qualities of a person who knows how to interact with other people in a way that inspires them to be their best.

I met Brian almost a decade ago. We became instant friends. We had "entrepreneur" in common. And our success motors were spinning at red line revolutions.

After Brian sold his online employment business, we met, and he shared with me his passion to become a professional speaker. I explained that professional speakers were pretty much stuffy – why don't we just stick to being amateurs, and inspiring audiences.

In four years, Brian Parsley has become one of the most dynamic amateur/professional speakers in the country.

This book is a reflection of his thought process, and a challenge to any leader or manager of people to think about human capital in new, exciting, and profitable ways. Novel ways.

This is not a book to read once and put down, this is a book to be studied, and its principles shared and implemented as quickly as possible.

Everyone in business wants to keep their customers loyal. But the bigger challenge is to keep employees loyal. Happy productive employees breed loyal actions to customers. For years I have told my audiences: **"Treat your employees better than you treat your customers."** That is at the core of what you will learn from reading Brian Parsley's book.

As leader, or manager, or coach, or teacher, you have a responsibility to help others be their best.

I promise that if you take the principles of this book and apply them, that the word BEST will become everyday practice at your company, with your people, and ultimately with your customers.

This book is inspiring. But it's up to you to read it, implement it, and be inspHIREd yourself.

– *Jeffrey Gitomer*
Author of The Little Red Book of Selling *and* The Little Red Book of Sales Answers

"Being a dynamic leader requires the ability to balance one's personal and professional life. I have seen Brian Parsley live out this balance in his own life and now he has beautifully illustrated these principles in Insphired. I highly recommend that those in positions of leadership read this book and dare to be different."

– James H. Morgan
Chairman of the Board, Krispy Kreme

"When it comes to identifying, hiring, and retaining employees, Brian Parsley's insight into hiring and retaining employees is akin to Newton's first mathematical for mulation of gravity."

– Todd Stancombe
President, Enventys

"*InspHIREd* is a great read and real time guide for all of us who truly understand that your business is only as strong as the people."

– Kenya V. Todd
HR Director, Choice Point

"There are books that tell you 'how' to hire, but this is the first to show you 'why.' *InspHIREd* is a book that is practical in application, but really helps you understand how Human Capital drives profit to the bottom line."

– Lewis F. Semones
Former President,
Wachovia Securities

"The wrong hire could cost our business millions in lost revenue each year. *InsHIREd* has given me new philosophies that I can implement immediately to avoid these potential mistakes."

– Bob Tyson III
Senior Vice President, Fidelity & Trust Bank

"Many books give us answers … the problem is, we don't know the questions! *InspHIREd* can teach you to ask the right questions … *InspHIREd* is a must read!"

– Donald L. Kosler
National Sales Manager,
Video Products Distributors

inspHIREd
Table of Contents

InspHIREd is not an HR handbook, or even a book that just tells you how to hire. The purpose is to tell you why and how to become a more effective leader. Whether you're currently a CEO of an organization, or one day aspire to become a great leader, this book will teach new philosophies, help you to understand your beliefs, and learn how to put them into action. Most people think they know how to hire, and they believe they know how to inspire, but reality says something different. Most people think they're great leaders (most people with body odor think they smell good too). Set aside your current belief system and how you think you should be a leader. Incorporate the principles of this book into your career and you will walk away with a renewed outlook on not just your work, but also your life.

1. What is SMART What is Dumb?

Anyone can make a hire, but hiring SMART is the key to employee loyalty, customer loyalty and company success.

SMART is an FLA (five-letter acronym): Smart Managers Always Retain Talent.

When you think or say "smart" in reference to employees, always think of this FLA. If you don't, you'll wonder why the greatest people in the world (that you hire) become lazy, complacent, rude, negative, and sloppy. Smart managers retain talent because they choose the right people from the start.

Hiring SMART, as opposed to hiring dumb, is the key to employee loyalty, customer loyalty, and company success.

Hiring SMART is how you begin to make a difference.

Smart – Characterized by sharp quick thought; bright; amusingly clever; witty.

Being smart means being bright, and being prepared to make the best choice or decision. It also means you're ready to make fast decisions based on the intelligent thoughts you've already developed in your mind.

But to hire smart – you gotta know what to avoid, and you've gotta know what's dumb.
What is dumb? Well, besides being "unintelligent" it just means you have made (or make) haphazard choices based on the current problem that needs to be solved.

Dumb – Conspicuously unintelligent; stupid; haphazard.

How many times have you heard of a manager who hires people because the company is behind in work? Or maybe, you've done it yourself!

It happens every day: choosing to make unintelligent, haphazard judgments based on an immediate need. The impact these type of decisions have on the bottom line is irreplaceable.

Want to get a return from your people? **(Your most important asset.)** Of course you do! The question is – how do you ensure it, and how do you measure it?

Choosing to hire SMART will help you top-grade your staff and assist you in making intelligent decisions when dealing with the human capital element of your organization.

Now is the time to take action!

2. The Seven Sins of Hiring, Inspiring, and Retaining Loyal Employees

Hiring in a crunch is like managing by crisis.

Let's face it – your intent is to hire the brightest and friendliest people every time. When actually making a hire, however, you're often hoping deep down that you don't make a major mistake. You interview and ask the same questions you've always been told to ask, but it seems you'd have better odds at a Las Vegas casino. How are you supposed to know how these people are going to perform in six months? How are you going to find out how these people conduct themselves under pressure? And most importantly, how are you going to know what their "work ethic" will be once the honeymoon phase is over? The answers to these questions can be found once you identify potential sins you have been committing BEFORE you hire someone.

After interviewing hundreds of hiring managers, and reflecting on my own experiences, I've found seven common hiring mistakes. If you've made these mistakes, it does not mean you are a lousy interviewer. However, if you notice a mistake you have made and continue to make it – well let's just say you'll get what you deserve.

7 Sins Hiring Managers Commit:

1. *Looking in the wrong place or at the wrong time.*
Do you find yourself only hiring or looking to hire when there is a need? This is a major mistake! Hiring in a crunch is like managing by crisis. Try looking for people you want before you have a need. If you need a great salesperson, you're probably not going to find them in the classifieds. They're already working for your competition. You need to solicit the best people in your industry. Get to know people who want to work in your organization. Network continuously, and be alert.

2. *Asking dumb questions.*
What kind of questions do you ask when you interview? "What are two strengths and two weaknesses you have?" or perhaps "What is your ideal work environment?" Do these sound familiar? Most hiring managers ask these, and other dumb questions, because that is the way they were taught. Try asking questions that engage the candidate to think. Now there's a new concept! Ask scenario-based questions, which walk a candidate through a potential situation. This will give you insight on how they will respond on the job. For example, "If a customer calls with a problem and you realize it's not your area of expertise,

how do you handle the call?"
I want to hear them give me solutions and ideas on how to serve the customer with a follow-up strategy. I don't want to hear them say things like "transfer" the call. The way they respond to these questions will give you some insight into how they will react in the real world.

3. *Making an offer just because you "need" someone.*
How many times have you made an offer to someone you know is not the best person for the job? Too many times hiring managers think that making a hire, even if they know they haven't found the best person for the job, will solve their immediate problems. It may solve immediate problems, but a new set of igger problems is right around the corner. Guaranteed. Be patient. Fill the position with the best candidate possible.

4. *Not setting clear expectations.*
Even though you understand the expectations in your company, your new employee may not understand them. Ask them to explain what they think their responsibilities are – so you know they understand. Taking this extra step in the beginning will eliminate confusion and frustration in the future. Setting expectations means explaining potential roadblocks, in addition to just stating company policies.

5. *Forgetting to reward employees.*
Every human being has three basic needs that must be fulfilled before they can feel valued. They need to be liked. They need to feel appreciated. And they need to feel important. There is no reward you can give to

make an employee feel valued if you are unable to meet these basic needs. You can give a cash bonus, but if you don't show appreciation, the employee will leave. You can give trophies, but if you fail to make your people feel like part of the team, they'll definitely leave you. Rewards are great, as long as they align with the three basic needs.

6. *Communicating poorly.*
Too many hiring managers assume they're communicating effectively with their employees. Never assume! Always ask the employee to repeat the issue to be sure they understand. You must also be sure to communicate with your employees regularly, whether communicating bad or good new. When employees feel involved, they feel appreciated. Communication, whether effective or ineffective, is integral in determining an employee's fate.

7. *Failing to create loyal employees.*
Loyalty is determined by your actions or inactions when an employee has a problem. The way you respond to problems will show everyone how you feel about your employees. When employees are loyal, they don't steal, cover up, make excuses, or use inflexible policies as a justification for poor customer service. And most importantly – they don't leave the company. Loyal employees create ongoing profits.

These seven sins are committed every day, all over the world, by hiring managers. If you avoid these sins, amazing things will occur. You'll hire the best employees, production will increase, morale will improve, and you'll see greater profits. No one starts a job to get fired or quit, but employees leave companies every day because managers fail them. Begin making smarter hires right now to ensure a better future.

3. Do you ask "Miss America" questions when interviewing?

Listen and you will learn

What type of questions do you ask when you are interviewing a candidate? For example, Asking dumb questions. "Name two strengths and two weaknesses you have?" or perhaps "Describe your ideal environment?" Most hiring managers ask these and other "Miss America" questions because that's what they were taught to do. The questions are so high-level and vague that you will rarely find a unique answer.

Begin by asking yourself these three questions:

1. *"Can they do the job?"*
What you really need to know is if they possess the technical knowledge to perform the tasks you give them.

2. *"Will they continue to do the job after they start?"*
It is one thing to possess the skills and it is an entirely different thing to maintain the drive to work hard. Most people achieve great success when they start a new job because of the passion!

3. *"Does job align with their soul?"*
If they hate animals and you own a pet store, then perhaps you need to stop fooling yourself into believing their skills will outweigh their "soul". That is why scenario questions are critical in hiring the right people. For example, you might say, "A customer calls you about a problem they're having and you realize it's not your account. How do you handle that type of call?" Listen carefully to the response you get. Would they transfer the call to someone else? Would they take the customer's problem, find a solution, and respond directly to the customer? I don't know what the right answer is for your business, but you do. Evaluate whether or not the answers align with your expectations. Think of potential scenarios that have happened or could happen in your business, create questions based on those scenarios, and incorporate those into your interview. It is also important to find out if the candidate fits into your culture. You may not think this is important, but you don't just want to build a team atmosphere – you want to create a family atmosphere. Families are far more valuable than teams. Don't just ask rote questions take down an answer. Ask why. Find out more about why someone thinks the way they do.

The questions you ask are incredibly important to the success of your business. Asking "Miss America" questions will make both of you feel good, but does little to add security to your bottom line. When you ask a scenario question or ask why they believe something, be ready to look hard at the response to see if it aligns with your beliefs, your values, and what you need in your business. Selecting the best employee is key. Don't just look for skills; look for people who can relate to others and add value to your business.

Expecting excellence of your employees starts with the interview questions. Have you ever heard someone say, "My employees are lazy"? It's not that employees are inherently lazy; it's that most people's lives are a reflection of the expectations of their direct peer group and supervisors. No one likes problems, but we all love challenges. It is important to challenge candidates during the interview process to see how they react and respond. People are constantly pushed outside of their normal operating procedures, and how they handle those situations will determine whether your business wins or loses.

4. Gut versus Testing

Have you ever made a hire that seemed to be perfect? They answered all the questions the way you hoped. They asked a lot of questions about the position. They had superb references. They looked the part. They came early. All of these are great and your gut said, "I should make this hire." You do, and a month later it seems like that same person transformed into a monster. They have a bad attitude. They don't provide the level of service they said was important when you first met them. What happened? You went with your gut instinct.

It happens all the time when hiring. We hear candidates say something and convince ourselves it's the correct answer. Think about specific questions you should be asking, but ask yourself if there is a better way to make a hire. Remember the saying, "You hire for skill, but fire for attitude." It is important that you find hard skills such as job competency; however, it's more important to understand how that candidate chooses to communicate.

Regardless of the position, the ability to effectively communicate is the difference between success and failure. Why is communication not the majority of the interview? You are too focused on what software programs they know or how many years they have worked in the industry. When a candidate gives you a list of references, how many are negative? There's a surprise! Don't you think you should take off the interview hat and get real?

I recommend having candidates take some type of behavioral assessment. There are many different types and which one you choose is very important. Choose one that does not measure personality traits. Personality traits are things like "loves dogs" and "enjoys beautiful days". How someone will behave or communicate is far more important to your business. The best assessments should have validity studies that back up the results. In addition, they need to be used as more than just a binary hiring tool. In other words, don't solely rely on a behavioral assessment to decide whether or not to hire a particular candidate.

These assessments should complement your gut feeling and help you look beyond the "honeymoon" period. Use assessment testing to help you communicate and work with the person after the hire is made. I personally recommend the DISC behavioral assessment, but you can find the one that is best suited to you and your business.

Using your gut is an important tool, but be certain you are making an educated decision and taking other factors into account. Testing for technical skills or knowledge is key for doing the job, but testing or assessing one's ability to communicate is a critical piece often overlooked. Assessments help filter out the potential lies (or perhaps the fluffy details) someone may say to you to give a false sense of security. You can only make a gut decision based on the information you have. Start hiring SMART by making informative choices based on qualitative and quantitative data.

5. Don't Train – Educate!

Training is important. It gives your employees the opportunity to learn techniques and processes.

But the key to effective training is to continue it indefinitely, enabling knowledge retention. This means you're not just training your employees. You're educating them.

An education will last forever. An education will be passed on to others. By educating your people, you will create a legacy.

I'm sure you've heard the expression "Teach a man to fish." That's a very impersonal way to look at the value of teaching. Maybe if the expression were "Teach your son or your daughter to fish," or "Teach your grandson or your granddaughter to fish," then you would realize the passion you have to have behind your teaching process. You would understand the patience you must have when teaching, and the encouragement you must give to your student in order to transfer your valuable information.

If you're looking to leave a legacy, then it's up to you to be able to create it – and then transfer it.

Best-selling author Jeffrey Gitomer once asked me, "Would you prefer your daughter have sex training or sex education?" Point well taken, Jeffrey. He went on to share with me that when you train, you show "how," when you educate, you show "why."

The key to extracting long-term results from your employees is educating them. They must understand their purpose, not just their job.

6. Human Capital Selection: The Key to Retention

If you hire dingbats and train them, you'll have a bunch of trained dingbats.

Look at retention as the return on your employee investment. People are assets to the organization and need to be treated as such. If your company owns 100 copy machines and none of them work, you have useless assets that bring zero value to the bottom line. No leader in their right mind would keep those copiers. In this same way, Human Capital is vital to the bottom line results of your company. Who you hire will determine your success or failure.

Hiring the best people is not quite as hard as you might think. First, you need to understand fully what this individual will be doing in your business. This needs to go much deeper than "they will answer the phones." That misperception is why you have turnover to begin with. If they, in fact, are expected to answer incoming calls, then find out who they would be speaking with (both internal and external). Understand specific scenarios they'll encounter each day in that position. Create or even modify the job description to include primary and secondary responsibilities. Being prepared, by understanding the position, will help you look for specific traits.

Pay the position – not necessarily by what the job title may suggest. Look at the impact this position could have on your bottom line. If this person answers your incoming calls, they hold the key to your vault. In fact, you could think of this person as your "Director of First Impressions." They can either create loyal customers for you, or they can help send customers to your competition.

When selecting people for your organization you need to interview SMART (Smart Managers Always Retain Talent). Spend less time focusing on technical knowledge, and more time on things that count. For example, how would they behave or act in stressful situations? What will happen when they have to deal with unreasonable people or customers? Too often managers focus on the skills and forget about the emotional side to hiring. Ask a lot of scenario-based questions.

Here is the tough part of this lesson: Shut up and listen! People keep talking as long as you let them. If you give them long enough, they'll tell you exactly how they will respond to real life problems you face each day. Listen and you'll gain invaluable insight on how well they would fit into your organization.

The key to selecting your employees is simple – take your time and focus on what's really important, not just what is urgent. This decision will impact your bottom line in one of two ways. The selection process is just as important as boardroom decisions. Start taking this responsibility seriously. Retention is the key to long-term success at your company. Be SMART and select wisely!

7. Interns: Are they valuable?

An increasing number of employers are using interns as a valuable resource from whom they can inject fresh input into their businesses. Many times interns are full of energy and have a lot of inspiring ideas. The glass ceiling or fears of longevity do not limit them. They want to learn, and they love to work! Interns can become one of your best resource pools for hiring and retaining loyal employees. Financially, they are the most cost-effective hire you will ever make. Many will work for little money and give you their heart and soul. In return, they seek knowledge and the ability to outperform their future competitors.

Don't mistake interns for "free labor," and certainly never hire interns as "eye candy" in the office. These individuals should be viewed as possible future assets. The bad news is, many interns are impressionable, so it's important to give them an environment that is safe and enjoyable. Never assume they understand everything even when they say they do.

They might just be the future leaders of your company.

I have heard that a lot of interns are lazy. "Lazy" is really only a reflection of the expectations given to them by you. Laziness is the symptom, not the disease. If you seek a hard-working, excited, energetic intern, then you have to expect excitement and work ethic.

Interns may appear to provide cheap labor, but they are the key to adding incredible value to your bottom line. Set the correct example and give an opportunity to someone who will give you the highest yield on your human capital investment.

8. The Real Rewards to Human Capital are Not Just Profits

I know you're in business to make money. There's nothing wrong with profits. There's nothing wrong with winning. But you should never compromise people for profits. The benefits are very temporary and always result in failure.

Let's say you purchase a lawnmower in the spring and use it daily for one year, but you neglect to maintain the machine. After one year you sell it to someone else. They use it a few times, and it begins to become unreliable. Eventually it stops working. They may think the machine is a lemon. They may think there is something inherently wrong with the machine. They are wrong, too.

The problem was caused by the person who purchased, used, and abused the machine by neglecting the maintenance. What do you expect when you take a new machine and force it to work the entire season without checking the oil, changing the filter, or replacing the spark plug? You're just asking for problems.

This same analogy is repeated each day in offices across the nation, probably in your office. You have employees that want to work hard. They come early and stay late and even take on tasks that are not considered normal job duties. But you neglect their needs. You don't involve them in the work that affects them. You stop filling their souls with encouragement and support. Why? Because they are just doing the job you paid them to do? Pathetic thinking.

If you invest in a regular lawnmower you may not consider it a big enough investment to take care of it regularly. But if you invest in a $300K one-of-a-kind lawnmower, I bet you would wipe it with a diaper after each use. This philosophy is all in your mind, not in your wallet. Output and profit are important to stay in business, but staying power is more important and it takes commitment to maintain.

When you invest in human capital you create a legacy – that's your real reward. You create and grow a family. It is about people, not just profits. You'll become richer than any Profit-and-Loss statement can ever show. Profits are the beautiful lawn you'll have from the hard work of you and your lawnmower. Treat it like you invested a lot, because you have.

Think of your job outside the realm of yourself and the company. Everyone has different reasons for doing things. Not everyone is working because they want to make a million dollars. Most people work because they have to – they have bills to pay or families to feed. These disparities in work ethics and values can greatly impact how you do business. It's important to discover why your people are working in the first place. For instance, if someone says they're in a job because they love money, is that bad? Not really.

Money lovers are not evil people. You should also understand that people don't love money; they love what it does for them. You need to find out why they love money. To find out what makes your people happy at work you must find out what makes them happy in life. Engage in dialog to discover what triggers their happiness. "What makes you happy?" "Why does it make you feel this way?" "Would you like to feel this way each day?" Is this really your job? Of course it is. You're a leader and that's what leaders do.

What does your job do for people? If you are in the mortgage industry you don't just do mortgages, you help people reach their dreams of owning a home. If you work at an airport you are moving the economy by helping business people reach their destinations to stimulate the growth in our country. If you're a teacher, don't forget you are impacting the future of many children who will never forget you. Is this idealism? I would challenge you to look deeper into this philosophy. Every small action will affect others. If you and your people are focused on the real reason you're in business, you will quickly see how this changes how you operate.

The real reward is not just profits; it's about doing what's right. It's about people. Your people. Start today by asking yourself, "Why am I here?" Then ask that same question to your people. Find ways to create memorable experiences with your people. Involve them in active dialog to discover ways to impact your customers' lives in everyday transactions. It is so easy. You'll be amazed at the results.

9. Key Elements to InspHIRE Your Employees

Motivation is temporary. Inspiration is permanent.

There is motivation, and then there is inspiration. Which do you think is better? Understanding the difference will create quantum leaps in your success.

You are motivated by your wants. You are motivated to make more money, get a raise, reach a goal, lose 10 pounds, and anything else you set your mind to.

But when you are inspired, great things happen. The Wright brothers were inspired to fly, and the great Martin Luther King, Jr., inspired millions of people to change the way they think about each other.

Remember:
Motivation is temporary.
Inspiration is permanent.

When you inspire your employees, you create loyal employees. Stop trying to motivate your people. Give them something to be proud of.

Here are four basic elements you can use to inspire your employees:

1. Give ownership.

Giving ownership doesn't mean giving equity or stock. It means you allow people to have ownership of the work that directly affects them and you give them the ability to make decisions that have a real impact on the company. You may have a hard time with this because you like to have complete control over what happens at your office.

Here's a question you can ask yourself to confirm my belief: "Do I allow my employees to make mistakes and teach themselves to develop solutions to these mistakes?" If you answered "No," then read carefully. The only way anyone can learn is by doing. If you want self-sufficient employees who can think on their own, and who will find solutions to problems (even if they create them) you need to give them the opportunity to learn. Don't just have them apologize for making the wrong decision – help them understand how to solve the problem. Allowing mental ownership is key to inspiring your employees.

2. Listen to what they think is important.

Often you spend the majority of your day putting out fires, returning calls, answering e-mails, and of course dealing with the politics of working with people. It is easy for you to focus your energy and attention on what is urgent. Many managers work all day and don't accomplish any real goals.

Don't make the mistake of doing what you think is important and ignoring your people. Challenge yourself to ask what your people think before you give your opinion. Involve them in your decision process as much as possible before making a final decision. This is important because it involves them in the work that affects them each day. The most effective way to show that you're listening is to take notes. This lets others know that you care and that what they're saying is important enough to write down. Listen and you will learn.

3. Reward effort, not just results.

When I say to reward effort and not just results, let me be very frank. I am not saying to reward failure. Understand that very few people have achieved greatness on the first try. Did Carl Lewis become the fastest human alive the first time he ran? Did Bill Gates wake up rich? People stop trying if they do not think they are growing or moving toward their goals. Some people persevere naturally, like Mr. Lewis and Mr. Gates. It really didn't matter what others thought, because they had the drive and the determination to reach their goals.

Not everyone is blessed with this sort of innate energy and drive. You need to reward people when they give all that they have. People don't have to be perfect, they need to be their best. Allow your employees to develop their skills, and reward them if their performance is innovative, exemplary, or team-oriented.

Whatever the circumstance may be, your job is to reward both large and small successes. The goal as a manager is to retain talent and generate the most output from your human capital. Motivation is temporary. Tap into the minds of your employees to see what rewards are important to them. Many times it may just be a verbal "great job." Keep them inspired and everyone will succeed.

4. Give praise in front of others.

Take time to mention and acknowledge specific events or stories of positive action – both privately and in front of others.

I have met managers who show appreciation by simply letting people keep their jobs. I have met others who give raises. How do you like to receive praise? How do you give praise to others? The two usually have the same answer. But the fact is, everyone is different. You must listen to your employees to find out what makes them feel valued.

Ask people what is important to them – how they feel about trophies, certificates, public praise, and monetary rewards. I think you will be surprised to find out that the majority of people in a working environment just want to feel appreciated. Money is a necessity, but most people crave recognition from their boss for their accomplishments.

Think of praise as the gasoline of the soul. You don't have to fill it up every day, but be careful about waiting until the red "warning" light comes on. You may get lucky the first couple of times, but eventually you run out of fuel. It is important to fill their souls with high-octane (praise-filled) fuel that will lead to their success – and yours. Listen to find out what makes your employees feel good and seek out ways to fill their souls every day. It doesn't need to be a big production, just a subtle reminder that you care.

These four basic elements will help you begin to inspire people. Motivation is key when you need to reach a short-term goal, but by itself it is worthless for achieving long-term success. The greatest leaders in history were inspirational. The secret is to find out what inspires those who work for you. Concentrate on their needs, not on what you think is important. Ask people what they want to achieve. When they speak, listen. Fill their career souls with appreciation (praise them) and strive to understand them. If you do this you will have inspired employees who will follow you to the ends of the world.

10. Recognizing Employee Signs and Symptoms – What to Look For and What to Look Out For

With the exception of food poising, people rarely get sick instantly. On the other hand, consider high cholesterol. Is it possible to eat a piece of cheese and instantly have high cholesterol? The answer of course is "no." High cholesterol is a chronic problem that can take years before signs and symptoms appear.

The same is true in your company. Bad customer service, company failure, and just plain slack employees take time to develop. Be cognizant of the shift towards mediocrity, and take action daily to prevent this deadly business disease. Just like in my medical example, we all know what will make us sick, and we still do it anyway. It is just easier to get caught up in the daily exercise of putting out fires and dealing with acute problems. We then put our corporate health on the back burner because we do not have the "pain" of the disease.

How do you know when you are getting a cold? Scratchy throat? Runny nose? Headache? These are symptoms that only you would recognize. A good doctor would look for and ask you about these symptoms to identify if there is a problem. Signs and symptoms can save your butt if you know what to look for. If you wait until the problem is obvious, you've probably waited too long.

Engage your employees regularly in discussion about the work that involves them. This will allow you to see if they are truly happy. The more you get to know someone, the more able you are to see subtle changes in their attitude or demeanor (symptoms) that can tip you off to something more serious (disease). By the time a person is an obvious wreck or upset, you will have to work 10 times harder to solve the problem.

Remember, you won't get healthy by eating just one carrot. Health, in your personal and work life, requires commitment.

11. Compensation: Too much? Not enough?

Whether you pay someone by the hour or on salary, you often ask yourself about the money. Everyone works the same hours (more or less), so how do you decide what to pay them? If you're fortunate enough to work for the government, they will tell you exactly what you're going to make and when you can go home.

Whatever you offer, employees always want more. How much is too much? This question is raised more often during performance reviews or annually because people have come to expect more money in relation to tenure. Nothing should be farther from the truth.

Here is an example:
If you pay an employee $12 an hour and then give them a 2% raise, they will be upset. If you give them a 10% raise they will think you are very generous. After six months they will not remember either of them. People forget about the increases because they want more. In America, people will almost always live a lifestyle that matches their level of income.

Stop focusing on the monetary part of compensation and begin focusing on the needs of your people. Surveys have proven that when most people do not enjoy their jobs and leave or quit, it is because of culture and NOT money. So why do you focus on the money? What kind of culture do you create for your company, business, department, or team? Do you even know what your people need in terms of emotional compensation? Remember the three basic human needs? Ask them what is important if you really want to know. Asking during an interview is ideal; however, you can always sit down with your current employees and get to know their needs.

Did you know some people only need you to recognize that they are working hard? Others require a little more attention, but fulfilling their emotional needs will cost your organization very little. It does require a commitment from you to follow through. There is a heavy investment of time that you must give in order to achieve the results you seek.

In a recent employee intervention with a client, we found that an entire branch was experiencing a downward turn in sales. The cause? Managers were arguing among themselves and were using employees as pawns in their power struggle. Employees were feeling pressure from the managers and began shutting down communication. As you can imagine, the customers were beginning to feel this same stress with the enforcement of policies and rules. The problem is, when stress begins to impact customers, they vote by taking their business next door. Everything you do will impact your bottom line, and it starts with compensation ...emotional compensation.

Begin asking people what is important to them (in addition to the basic need to earn a living). "What would you like to see happen at the office to make you feel more involved?" "If you could work towards any position here what would it be?" "What things do you do that people may overlook?" "What kind of ideas do you have that can help our customers refer others?"

What are you doing? Are you involving your employees in the work that directly affects them? Are you making them feel appreciated? Are you getting their commitment or emotional "buy-in" to your goals? Compensation is subjective. Of course money is an important part of the process, but not nearly as important as you. Your commitment to serving your employees by helping them feel involved will allow you the freedom to give more. Loyal, dedicated employees will create loyal customers, which in turn will generate incremental revenues. This will give you the opportunity to reward employees with more money because there will be more to give. It's a 360-degree process that begins with emotions, not dollars.

... Compensation is subjective. Of course money is an important part of the process, but not nearly as important as you. Your commitment to serving your employees by helping them feel involved will allow you the freedom to give more. Loyal, dedicated employees will create loyal customers, which in turn will generate incremental revenues. ...

12. The Loyalty Food Chain: How Employee Loyalty Leads to Company Profits

I'm always surprised when I meet with leaders of organizations who believe that success comes directly from marketing and the delivery of their products. I'm not sure if it is arrogance, greed, or just ignorance. If you want consistent profits you need loyal customers, period. And the only way you will retain loyal customers is by maintaining loyal employees.

Allow me to show you the loyalty food chain:

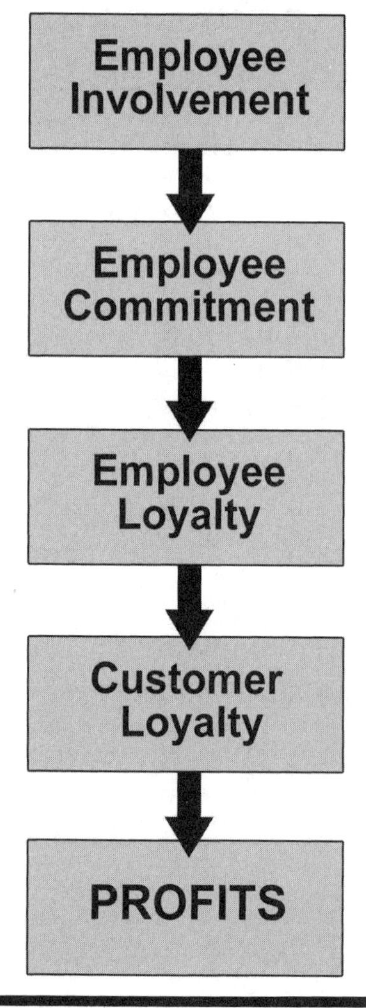

How do you achieve employee loyalty?

You begin by involving your people in the process of doing business. For instance, Job Descriptions. Everyone hates them! Does each employee have a copy of their own? Do you have a copy of yours? Even if you're part of the minority that does have a copy, you're not out of the woods.

You need to get the job descriptions (if you have any) and give them to each employee. Ask them to take the descriptions home and make any additions to their responsibilities, and delete items that either do not apply to their positions or are outdated. Of course share with them that you may not be able to make every change, but let them know that their input is very important for this process to work. After you receive the changes, meet with each employee or group with the same job description and review the findings. This is going to help strengthen your team, because you're directly involving your employees in the work that affects them. You're teaching them commitment and allowing them to "own" their jobs.

After you make the modifications to the job descriptions you will find that your employees will have a different level of commitment. This is because they buy into the program. It's very difficult to criticize the broccoli casserole when you baked it yourself. It is easy to blame "management" or any other vague entity when you are not accountable and committed. Involving employees is the genius of the loyalty food chain.

Who knows more about answering the switchboard – the CEO or the receptionist? If you said receptionist, then why are most managers telling the receptionist how to answer the phone? "Here is our phone policy." Here is another example to illustrate my point about involving the employee. Would it not make more sense to ask the receptionist about their job? Perhaps you need to find out what they think is important: How they transfer, place on hold, take messages, get back-up support, take lunch, and handle irate customers. You're too busy making policies to become more efficient. A good friend of mine who is a doctor said, "Before I treat, I must diagnose. But before I diagnose you must admit there is something wrong."

Denial is the biggest obstacle you will ever encounter at work or in your personal life. Many people don't even want to think that perhaps the problem lies within. Instead they blame others for the situation they're facing. What is my friend really saying? You must diagnose the problem and then figure out how to "treat" the problem. You rarely go to a doctor and tell him that you have a headache and he replies, "We must operate!" The doctor examines you and then takes steps to identify what the problem really is. This is why they "diagnose" you before making a decision. If you ignore the symptoms or decide you have nothing wrong with you, it may cost you your life. Involve your employees in processes so they can assist you in diagnosing potential cancers in the organization.

Let's talk about employee commitment. When do we see the highest level of employee commitment? The first day on the job! On that day, if someone asked an employee to take another job offer, would they take it? If someone asked them to call out sick, would they? If you needed them to stay late or take on additional responsibilities, do you think they would? Oh, and would they have a great attitude too? You bet they would – and then some. Unfortunately, this is often only temporary. Between policies and criticizing, they begin to lose this commitment. They have no control over their own destiny and thus find no need to stay committed.

If you ignored your spouse or significant other on a consistent basis and slowly discredited their ideas, what would happen? If you nagged and pointed everything they were doing wrong in the relationship, what would happen? They would leave you if they were smart. What happens with your employees? They leave you if they are smart. "There is no commitment if there is no involvement." Remember that. Making people feel like part of the family is the key ingredient in keeping a committed long-term employee.

If you can achieve employee loyalty, customer loyalty becomes a breeze. It is important to remember the food chain moves linearly approaches profits. The following story illustrates my point. I was staying at a hotel in Norfolk, Virginia on a business trip and had the following experience: I returned to my room and it had not yet been cleaned. No worries on my side because I was staying another night and who cares if my bed is made in the room? I noticed a cart outside of my door so I opened the door and told the housekeeper that she did not have to clean my room, but I would love to have a couple of towels. Her reply to me was, "You are not on my list so you need to call housekeeping if you want towels." Her tone was arrogant and condescending, but her soul was saying something else. I think she was saying to me, "I am so unhappy with my job because my employer does not allow me to do what I think is right. Instead, I have to do what they think is right. I have no control over what I do. Since this is an opportunity to have control, I will flex my decision muscle."

Because there was no employee loyalty, there was no customer loyalty. I have never returned to that hotel because of that experience. Both customer and employee loyalty are fostered by standards, but created by problems. Problems are our opportunities to create memorable experiences and to create loyalty.

Before you say anything negative about the experience I had, answer this question:

How do your employees speak to your customers? How do they speak to each other? Think you know? What about the managers of that hotel? Think they knew? If I pay for a product/service and it goes off without a hitch, I think nothing of it. But if there is a problem, how it is resolved or not resolved is what creates loyalty or mediocrity. Your actions and inactions are what dictate what happens in your company. I write about customer loyalty with employee loyalty because they both live in the same domain.

When I was on vacation in Jamaica I met a man who completely changed my perception of employee loyalty. Mr. Virgo works at a hotel as a driver for the guests. My wife and I had the pleasure of spending an entire day with Mr. Virgo as he drove us across Jamaica. What made Mr. Virgo so interesting was his story of loyalty to the company. Mr. Virgo walks 1.5 hours each way, to and from work, 6 days a week! Think about that next time you're stuck in traffic in your air-conditioned car when it is 92 degrees outside. But why does he spend all this time walking to and from work? Some would hypothesize that there are few jobs there and people are desperate for work. I guess that would answer the 1.5-hour walk each way, but what about his passion?

You see, Mr. Virgo told us that he gets to hear stories from people all over the world and learn about new things each day. He loves people and he loves his job. After we built rapport we began talking about money. Mr. Virgo has two little girls and a wife at home. He earns around $2 (U.S.) an hour. `He said, "Mr. Parsley, I live by this principle – give a little, save a little, and spend a little. If I had a different job making more money, I would not be able to meet great people like you."

I bet you're thinking Mr. Virgo was just being nice because he wanted a tip. Believe me, I have been around a lot of people who wanted tips and he was very genuine. In fact, on the day we were leaving the island, Mr. Virgo was waiting in the lobby to drive us to the airport. Not too odd, except for the fact that it was his only day off that week. He said he wanted to see us to the airport to ensure we had a safe journey. Amazing man, and the lessons I learned from him on that trip!

Why can't you become Mr. Virgo at least some of the time? What Mr. Virgo did was create a memorable experience for my wife and me. That memorable experience has created additional job security for Mr. Virgo because I have shared this story with thousands of people all over the country. In fact, some people, on my advice, have journeyed to that hotel and now have their own stories about Mr. Virgo. It does not matter what you do or what you earn, but rather what you can do to impact others. This is customer service. This creates loyalty! Your job is to create that type of family or passion in your organization.

This is the secret lesson in life we can all learn: Memorable experiences are what create our successes and failures in life and business.

Try this exercise: Name the last five Miss America pageant winners, and while you are at it, name the NFL Super Bowl champions from the 1980's in chronological order. Now name five friends who have helped you in some time of need in your lifetime. Or name some of your childhood neighbors. I bet you had no trouble answering the last two questions. You see, when we talk about great accomplishments, they are only memorable for a short while. Excellent, memorable service creates long-lasting (if not permanent) impressions in our lives. Using this assumption, how do we create loyal employees? How about loyal customers? In all my travels I have met a few people who have created these memorable events. There was Ms. Lorna, who drove my wife to the pharmacy in her personal car when the hotel van was not available. Also Jessica, a flight attendant on US Airways, who overheard me saying I was recently married and gave me a bottle of wine (this was especially cool because the policy was to not give away bottles). I have shared these stories with thousands of people because it is rare to receive this kind of service. I find that so amazing since we all crave this kind of attention. Everyone talks about it, but few give it. If people don't know better, they don't do better.

Without employee loyalty there will never be customer loyalty or company success. If you are a hiring manager, the decisions you make will affect the bottom line of the company every time. We have all heard the saying, "An organization is only as strong as its weakest link." This is never so true as when you speak about the impressions people in your organization make. If you go to a store for the first time and get the worst service you can imagine, what do you think? "Mary sure gave us bad service." Or would you think "That store has the worst service ever, and I'll never come back again!" That may sound extreme, but it happens every day and probably to your business. People will not remember your employees' names in most cases, but they will remember your company name.

Employee loyalty can create profits or losses for your business. The great news is, it's your choice! If you don't like what you see in all of your employees, look in the mirror. You either allow it or you teach it! It is called personal responsibility to your people. Don't even think about saying, "You don't understand, Brian." I understand it starts with whom you hire and how you treat your employees. If they are not capable of learning their job responsibilities or even worse, fitting into the culture that you want to create, then get rid of them. Help them get a job with your competitor.

The good news is you can create profits by hiring, inspiring, and retaining loyal employees.

As you learn new ways to hire, think of the loyalty food chain. When I show you better ways to inspire your people, think of the loyalty food chain. In fact, follow the loyalty food chain and you will have more profits – forever!

13. Passionate Employees Lead to Loyal Customers – and Profits!

You can't teach passion, but you can bring it out in people!

What is passion anyway? The scholars would say it's an "intense, driving, or overmastering feeling or conviction." The interesting thing about passion is you can't fake it. If you attempt to fake passion it's immediately seen as duplicitous behavior. This being said, you can't train someone to have passion either. If you hire dingbats and train them, you will have a lot of trained dingbats. You can, however, hire passionate people and foster an environment that will keep the passion from fading.

I was staying at a hotel in Palm Beach, Florida, and was window-shopping around 10 p.m. and I heard a gentleman address me from behind. He said, "Good evening, sir." I greeted the man as he cleaned cigarette butts from an ashtray. I thought to myself, "How nice of this gentleman to greet me." But before I could finish my thought he continued, "Sir, the gift shop does not reopen until 8 in the morning, so if that is inconvenient for you I would be pleased to get the key from the manager and allow you to get what you need. We can always just add it to your room bill." WOW!!!

What was that? In a world of mediocrity I was blown away. If he were the manager I would think "That's nice, but it's his job to offer that to his guests." One word could sum up what had just happened to me in the hall – PASSION! You see, they hired someone with a passion for serving others. Have you ever encountered a high-paid, passionless jerk? Money has nothing to do with passion and neither does a job title or responsibilities. I firmly believe you can't teach passion, but you can bring it out in people.

Remember your first day at a new job? You wake up early, get dressed, and smile from ear to ear all day. You sit at your new desk, put away your paper clips and set up your voicemail. Life is good, isn't it? What happens? The honeymoon ends and you begin to lose the passion and motivation you had. You wake up dreading going to work. Monday seems to come too quickly and Friday seems so far away.

Keep your employees' passion from fading. Create an environment that fuels their passion. I have found that employee involvement creates commitment. Commitment leads to passion. Passionate employees are loyal, and employee loyalty inevitably transfers to customer loyalty.

Loyal customers, not satisfied customers, are what lead to profits. Look up the meaning of "satisfied" and you'll find it's when a debt or obligation is paid in full. A satisfied customer will move to the next best thing for many reasons. But a loyal customer will never leave you unless you violate their trust. Loyal means dedicated to a person or ideal. This should change your thoughts when striving to create and maintain satisfied employees and customers.

14. The Difference Between "Team" and "Family"

Do you believe your company would be golden if you could create a "team" culture in your office?

When someone says the word "team," what comes to mind?

Sports? *Marriage*? WORK?

A team can accomplish more than a single person, in shorter periods of time. But take a look at the definition of team.

"Team - A group organized to work together;
a group on the same side, as in a game."

But just because we're on the "same side" and "work together," doesn't mean that success is ensured.

In fact, the team concept falls short if you want to create a dynamic organization. If you're winning, the team concept seems perfect. But what happens when times get tough? Suddenly the team shows weakness from all the stress.

Teams have their purpose, but they're an incomplete recipe for success in business. If a professional sports team does really well during the regular season and blows their shot at a championship, what happens?

Management may think the "team" wasn't as strong as they thought. Teams become temporary and are based on performance outcomes. I have seen organizations focus their entire hiring strategy on a specific goal and the "team" they need to hire to accomplish that goal. We seem to think this idea will work for us. But in reality, it's just a recipe for failure.

Take a look at a new way to think about your employees and co-workers. Begin to see employees and co-workers as a second family.

Have you ever told a friend you consider them family? "If you need anything at all, you can count on me. You're like family." See, it's a higher level of commitment between friends. If this "family" member (who by the way is not related legally) calls you at 3 o'clock in the morning for help in a crisis, would you immediately do anything you could to help? Of course you would!

Look at the definition of "family":
"Family - Two or more people who share goals and values, have long-term commitments to one another, and usually reside in the same dwelling place."

Does that sound like you and your fellow employees in an ideal work situation? At the least, you can relate to the part about residing in the same place (for 8 or more hours a day).

Imagine how much you could accomplish in a situation where your goals and values are shared with the people you interact with.

One of my clients is a national mortgage lender. When I started my relationship with them, I quickly recognized the family-like relationships among co-workers. At the time, it alarmed me.

I questioned whether that close of relations, in a business setting, could be dangerous. What if they get in a fight? Let someone go? How are they going to correct or punish their employees?

But with time, reality emerged, and I understood why the company is strong.

Their direction and success is based on their people - not just their goals.

People are motivated by goals and driven by people.

The CEO created a family culture that empowers their people to set high standards of care - both for their customers, and for their co-workers.

How do you create a family environment in your business setting? How will you create a family environment if your current organization is not a team now?

Creating a family at work means you must have trust, open communication, desire to serve, and follow-through. And it means each "family member" will have these characteristics, or will be willing to learn them.

Your job is to create a culture that will teach people. Your job is to provide a culture that will leave a legacy with your employees. Your job is to find pleasure in coming to work. Your job is to help others find that same pleasure.

In a family culture, people are more willing to go to bat, to protect and to serve one another as opposed to creating barriers between individuals.

Focus your energies on how to create "my family" at work, rather than meeting this quarter's goals - and long-term success will happen.

15. The Cost of Lost

There is a quantitative metric you can use to figure out how much money it costs your bottom line when you turn over an employee. Many leaders don't realize that a $10 an hour employee can cost $8,000 to turn over. With that in mind - you can extrapolate the cost of your salaried people.

What are these costs? Recruitment, training, low productivity of a new hire, and the biggest one of all - "lost sales" cost, or opportunity cost.

Then there is an even bigger cost! It is called the "hidden cost" of a lost employee. Hidden costs affect your morale in the office. These include the fear and uncertainty that people begin whispering about when you are not around. When turnover happens, it is critical for you to communicate the impact with the peers of the departing employee. This applies to voluntary and involuntary turnover. You must involve the employees in understanding the purpose of the decision.

I am not suggesting you reveal confidential information. Rather, I am recommending that you explain how the change may or may not affect each individual. You may think that it's none of their business (which may be true), but it is in your best interest to educate them and put your spin on the situation before rumors begin.

You need to understand that achieving zero turnover is not a reasonable goal to achieve. Turnover is inevitable regardless of what you say or do. In fact, some turnover is good to have within your organization. You should always try to top-grade your people and have them push themselves to become great. New employees bring new ideas and abilities that will help you get to the next level.

16. Why People Quit

We want to believe that people quit their job because they have found a better opportunity, but the real reason they quit is because of bad leadership.

You make the decision on how you choose to manage. It's in your best financial interest to understand what your employees' needs are, and then to meet these needs. I bet you can think of a passive job seeker (or two) in your own office. These are people who may not have their resume out in the public domain, but would leave you in a second if the right offer came along.

We always want to believe people quit because they have found a "better" opportunity (they'll be able to earn twice the money with half the work doing the same job somewhere else, or they need better benefits or more of a challenge). But the real reason people quit is because of bad leadership.

A study from the Saratoga Institute analyzed 60,000 exit interviews and found that 80% of people left their job because of bad management. That statistic is staggering!

Have you ever had a bad manager? Did you leave your work because of it? Or an even harder question: are you a bad manager yourself? Do you think the bad manager you had in your career thought of themselves as bad? Do you think of yourself as bad? Unfortunately, we see the world as we think we are, not as it really is.

Managers spend too much time focusing on numbers, deadlines, goals, and production, when instead they should be putting their people first (so the numbers can take care of themselves). It is important to treat your people with the same level of respect with which you would treat your own child. Give support and reward small successes. Teach your people a different way, don't just tell them "how it is". Don't just bark orders, explain why you are making a decision and give your employees the opportunity to fully understand.

How you manage is highly important to your ability to retain loyal employees - and determines whether or not your people will quit. Don't wait to react. Take charge now!

If you fear losing a specific person, money is NOT the secret to keeping them. We have already learned that all people have the same basic human needs: to be liked, to feel important, and to be appreciated. Sometimes money complements your efforts, but monetary compensation should never be seen as the cure-all.

There are people that quit and find other jobs, and there are people that quit and just keep showing up to work. Get more involved if you want lower turnover. Understand that turnover is not bad, but the cost of lost is great if you don't understand why this has happened.

17. The SMART Way to Fire an Employee

This book is not intended to give you legal advice. If you are uncertain about any employment laws in your specific area or industry, you should seek legal counsel. With that being said, there is a SMART way to fire an employee.

If you have never had the "privilege" of letting someone go, you probably will. It is emotional and arduous because no one wants to hurt someone.

Here is the SMART way to let an employee go:

1. Put yourself in their shoes.
They might not know it's coming and have no clue that the multiple warnings were a precursor to this day. Try to understand how this will impact them and their family. I believe it will help you become a little more empathetic to know what is going through their mind so you can soften the message when it is delivered.

2. Give dignity.
I remember getting fired once, and it made me feel worthless. There is really no value in kicking someone when they are down. Even if you are correct in firing them you should always treat them with dignity. Remember, someone hired them in the first place. It

has nothing to do with karma and everything to do with what's right.

Remember, there is law - and there is humanity. Do what is right and you will become a more effective leader.

18. Finding Your "Soul Career"

If someone told you that you were going to die in five years, what would you choose to do for a living? What would you want to accomplish before then? Would you leave a legacy? Would you pay off your credit card debt? These are important reflections because it may not be what you are doing now. Why aren't you choosing to live your best life now?

People spend their whole lives trying to find purpose.

Can you find your "soul career" the same way you find a soul mate? And what is this "soul career?" You find your "soul career" when you're doing what makes you happy - and what you know is right to do. When you're in your "soul career" you'll feel a strong, deep emotion of purpose that reaches your vital core and allows you to find purpose at work.

Are you still searching for your "soul career?"

Here is how to begin searching for your "soul career." Write a list of the things that make you genuinely happy. Don't just say lots of money or financial success. Financial success without the feeling of fulfillment is failure. Why would you want financial success? Is it because you want a million pieces of green paper that represent a million dollars? Or is it because financial success gives you choices, security, and freedom?

You need to understand the real reasons why you want things. Challenge yourself to understand what really makes you happy. And then write it down. Write down what motivates and drives you. Be as specific as possible when doing this exercise.

Now write a separate list of things that have special meaning to you. These are the things that fulfill your soul. These are the core values you live by each day. Also write down what makes you feel as though you will leave a legacy.

Take a look at the two lists together. When you find where your two lists intersect - you will find the basis of your "soul career." It's a combination of the things that make you happy and the things that have a deep meaning to you.

What are you willing to give up to reach the point of intersection? The proposition is creating a lifestyle that transcends from work to your personal life. How do you create a lifestyle that transcends from your work to your personal life? A commitment to finding these answers will enhance your life and give you purpose. Define your "soul career" and create a plan to achieve it. Here's an example: if you have a genuine desire to help and serve others you wouldn't be a good con-artist. Perhaps you love the idea of transferring knowledge to others. Your best fit would be teaching, coaching, or management.

I am not suggesting you quit your job and move to the beach to surf because you love surfing. What I am saying is make certain you uncover what your motivating factors are, so you can align your work style to fit neatly with your personal style.

Focus your lifestyle on specific principles that you can apply to everyday life. Your job is to be a better person and to lead people with your actions.

Your principles should start with integrity, honor, and ethics. They should follow the concept of creating a family at work and creating friendships with customers. These should not seem like chores, rather they should be intrinsic values that align with your soul. Re-capture that passion you had on your first day on the job! It's difficult because it requires commitment and diligence.

It is easy to maintain a job and get a paycheck. It is hard to love your work and become proud of what you do each day

As a manager, what do you really want? If you desire loyalty from others, you must first give loyalty to others. Enjoy the life you have, find your purpose and stop waiting for "someday." Commitment to finding your purpose in life will bring you a sense of fulfillment that you can't get in a bottle or pill. Life is too long to be miserable. It is time to take charge of your own destiny by taking this new knowledge and putting it into action.

You now understand not only how to create loyal employees, but you understand why. There is one thing that separates the doers from the talkers, and that is taking action. The time is now. Commit to a new lifestyle. Take it to work with you. Find the success you want, and be happy - as you deserve.

Notes of inspHIREation

Notes of inspHIREation

Notes of inspHIREation

Notes of inspHIREation

It is important I thank the following people for their support and help in making this book the best it could be.

Michelle. Thank you for helping me with the title and for understanding what I was trying to create.

Liz. Thank you for the many hours of hard work you put into this book. You worked late into the night and never complained. You took pride in the project, and it shows.

Jessica. Thank you for using your talents to help me deliver a product that was far above my expectations. I am sure thousands of leaders will appreciate what you did to make it easy for them to read and understand.

Brian Parsley is a Certified Professional Behavioral Analyst and a Human Capital Strategist who speaks to companies on sales, customer loyalty, and employee retention. Brian's seminars provide real-world insights into the connection between employee behavior and bottom-line results.

Brian is the President of TrainOne, Inc. (www.trainone.com). He works with businesses to develop best practices, and helps managers create office cultures that retain employees, keep customers loyal, and increase revenue by serving the needs of customers.

He also served as Chairman of the national online recruitment site, USAhire.com.

Brian was recently named one of Charlotte, North Carolina's top 40 executives under 40 years old.

Your company can be
inspHIREd
by Brian too.

For more information call 704.333.1112
or email brian@trainone.com